Activating the Promises of God through Prayer

— Journal & Notebook —

by

debby gautreaux

Published by:

McDougal & Associates
18896 Greenwell Springs Road
Greenwell Springs, LA 70739
www.thepublishedword.com

McDougal & Associates is an organization dedicated to the spreading the Gospel of the Lord Jesus Christ to as many people as possible in the shortest time possible.

ISBN: 978-1-950398-47-8

Printed on demand in the U.S., the U.K. and Australia
For Worldwide Distribution

Introduction

Thank you, woman of God, for purchasing my book and Journal. I am so excited by what God is going to do and say to you as you read the book and work through the journal. Hopefully, one day you can look back on it and see how God has answered your prayers.

I believe God cares about even the most detailed things about you and wants you to speak to Him about your every need. You are so precious to Him. He cares about your every need. He cares about your family, what job you will take, your bills, your health, your prayer life. He even cares about everyone in your family, just as much as you do.

Never forget that your prayers matter. I know that God can't wait for you to speak to Him.

As an intercessor, sometimes God will have me just tell Him things that are on my heart, things that matter the most to me. It's not just about prophetic declaring and praying prayers of warfare. Sometimes we just need to pour our burdens onto Him and give Him everything, so we don't get too burdened down by life. Just let it go and let God. Then put it in the journal as a record of what you have done, close the book, and walk away. When you do this, you will see God answering your prayers. It's just that simple.

So, thank you again, and may God bless you in everything you set out to do for Him.

In Him,
Debby Gautreaux

The smoke of the incense,
mixed with the prayers
of God's holy people,
ascended up to God from the altar
where the angel had poured them out.
— Revelation 8:4

Activating the Promises of God through Prayer

Prayer Journal

Intercession

But when you pray, go into your room, close the door and pray to your Father who is unseen. Then your father, who sees what is done in secret, will reward you.   Mathew 6:6

(Some translations say *"openly reward you."*)

Prayer Journal

_____
_____
_____
_____
_____
_____
_____
_____
_____
_____
_____
_____
_____
_____
_____
_____

Intercession—"the act of intervening on behalf of another"
Prayer Journal

_____
_____
_____
_____
_____
_____
_____
_____
_____
_____
_____
_____
_____
_____
_____
_____
_____
_____
_____
_____
_____
_____
_____
_____
_____
_____
_____
_____

A Prayer Journal

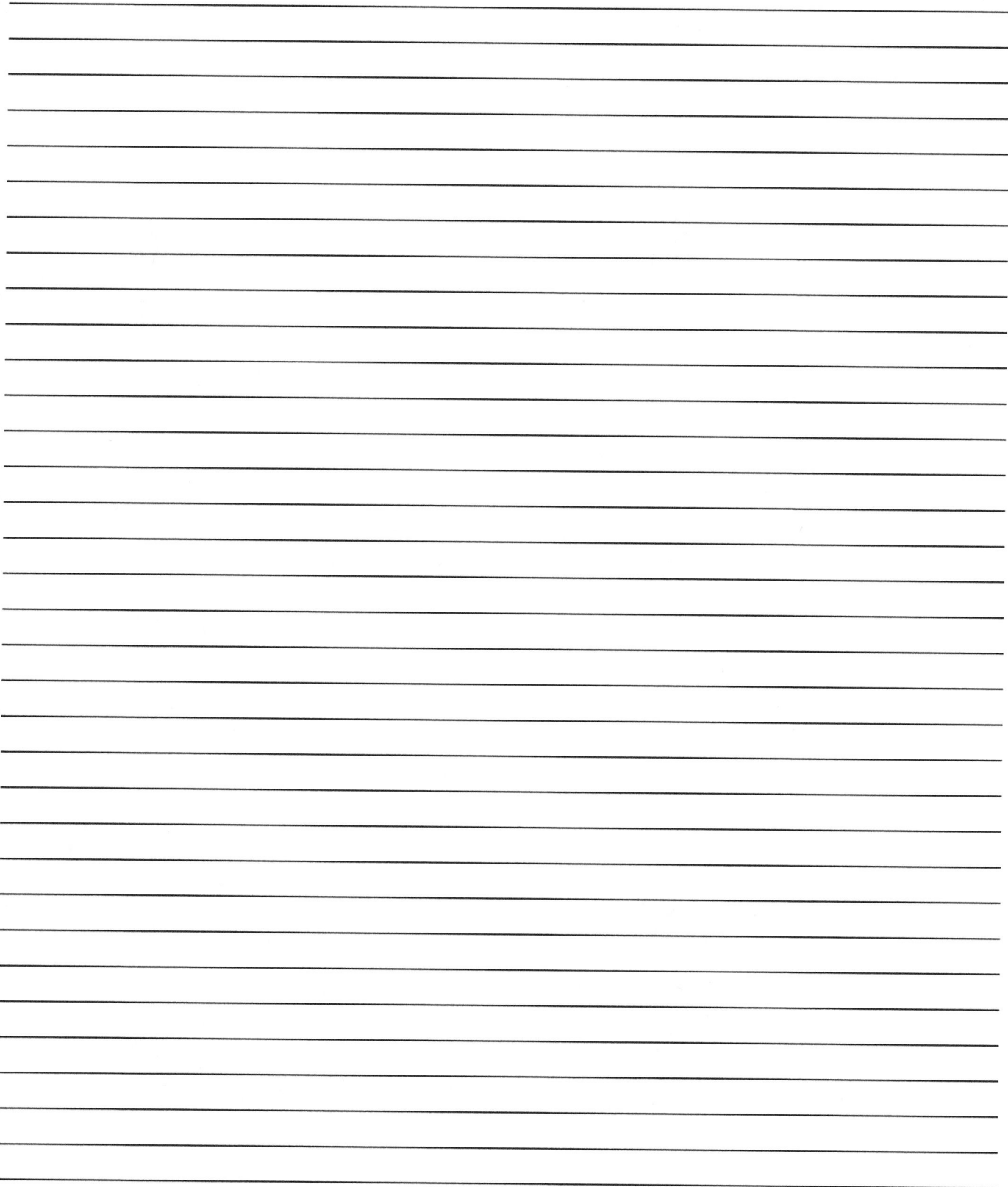

I am a Woman of God

A Prayer Journal

Seek God

A Prayer Journal

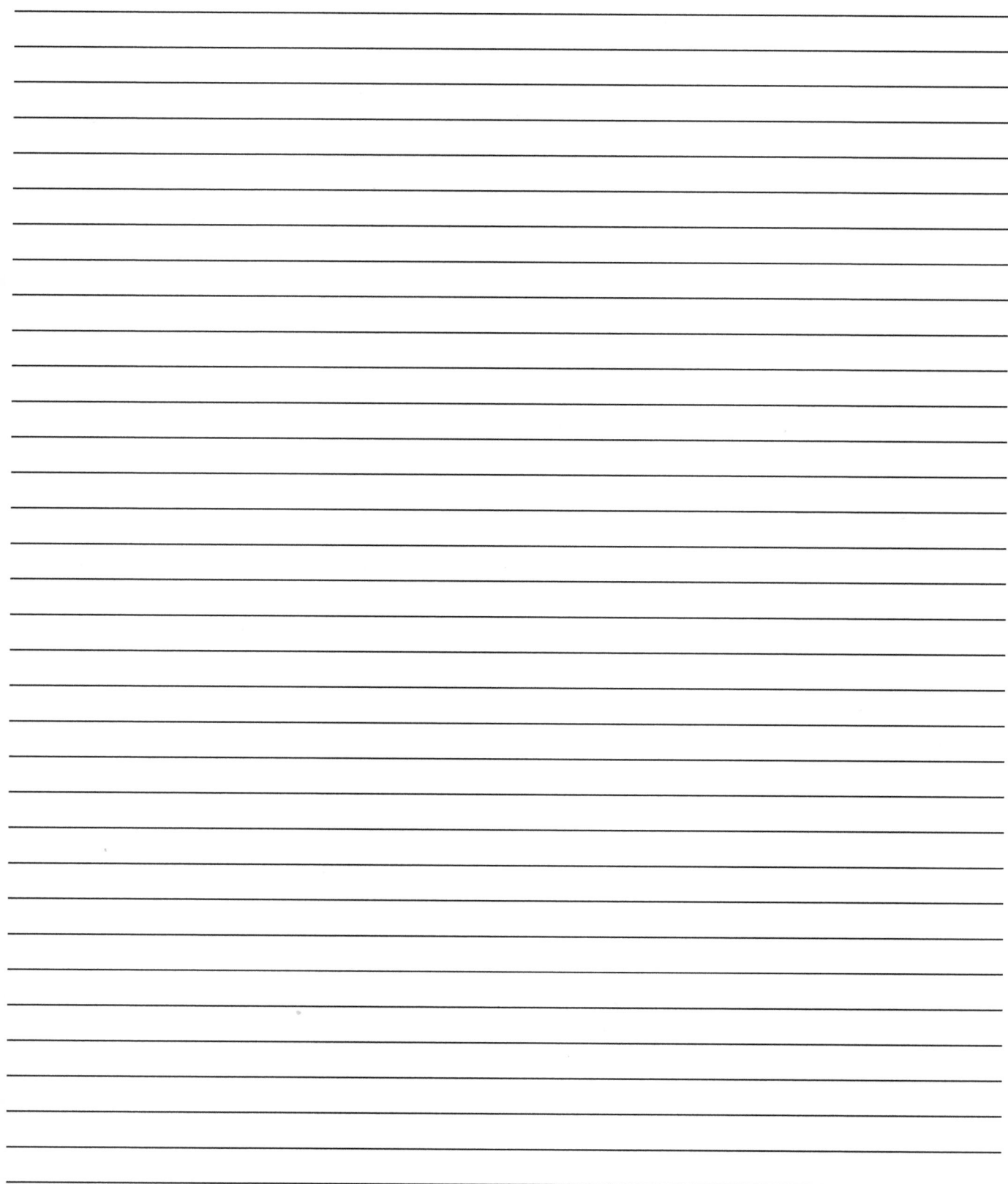

A Prayer of Thanksgiving
Giving God All the Glory

A Prayer Journal

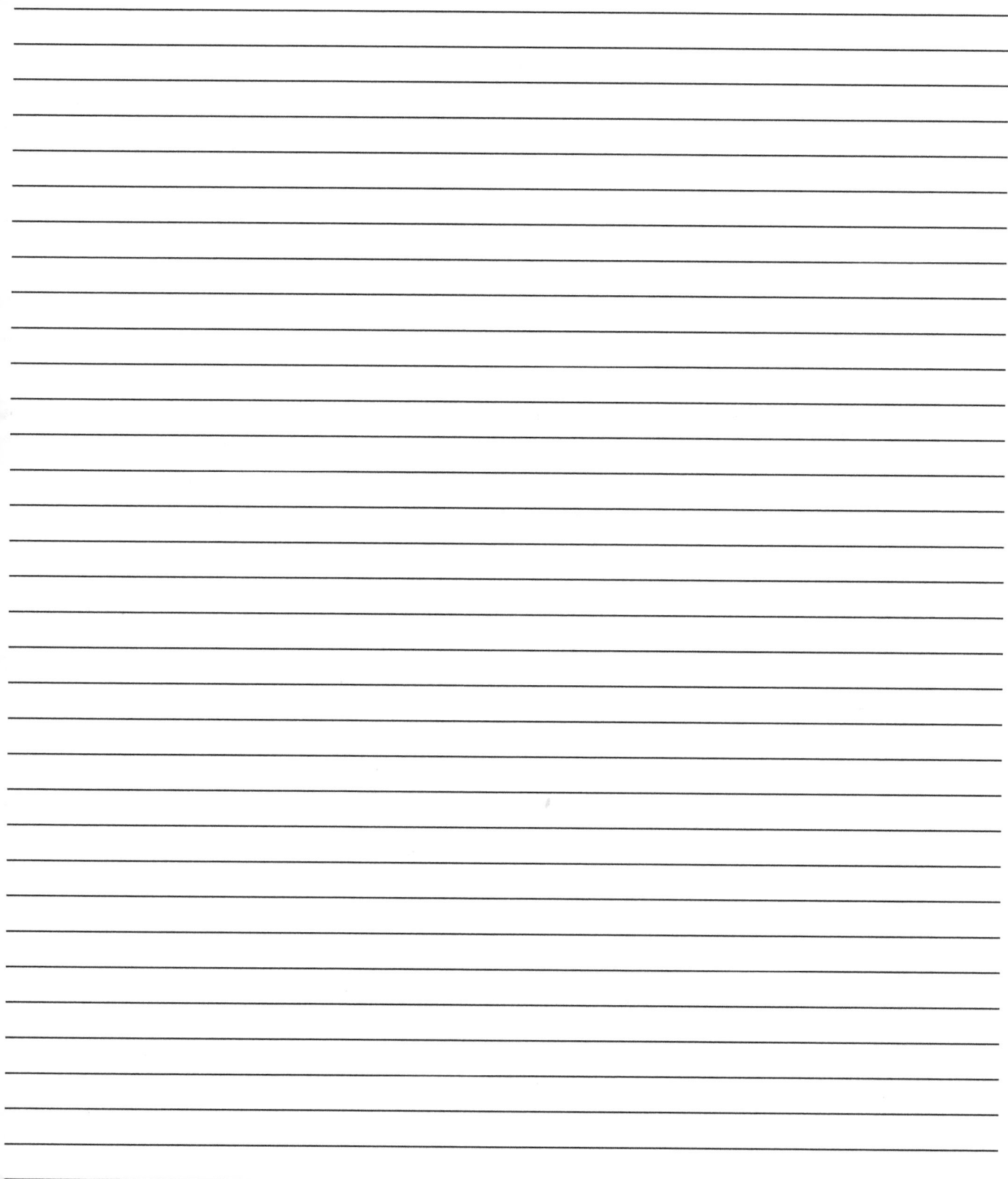

Enter His Gates with Thanksgiving

Let Us Pray

Thankful Expression

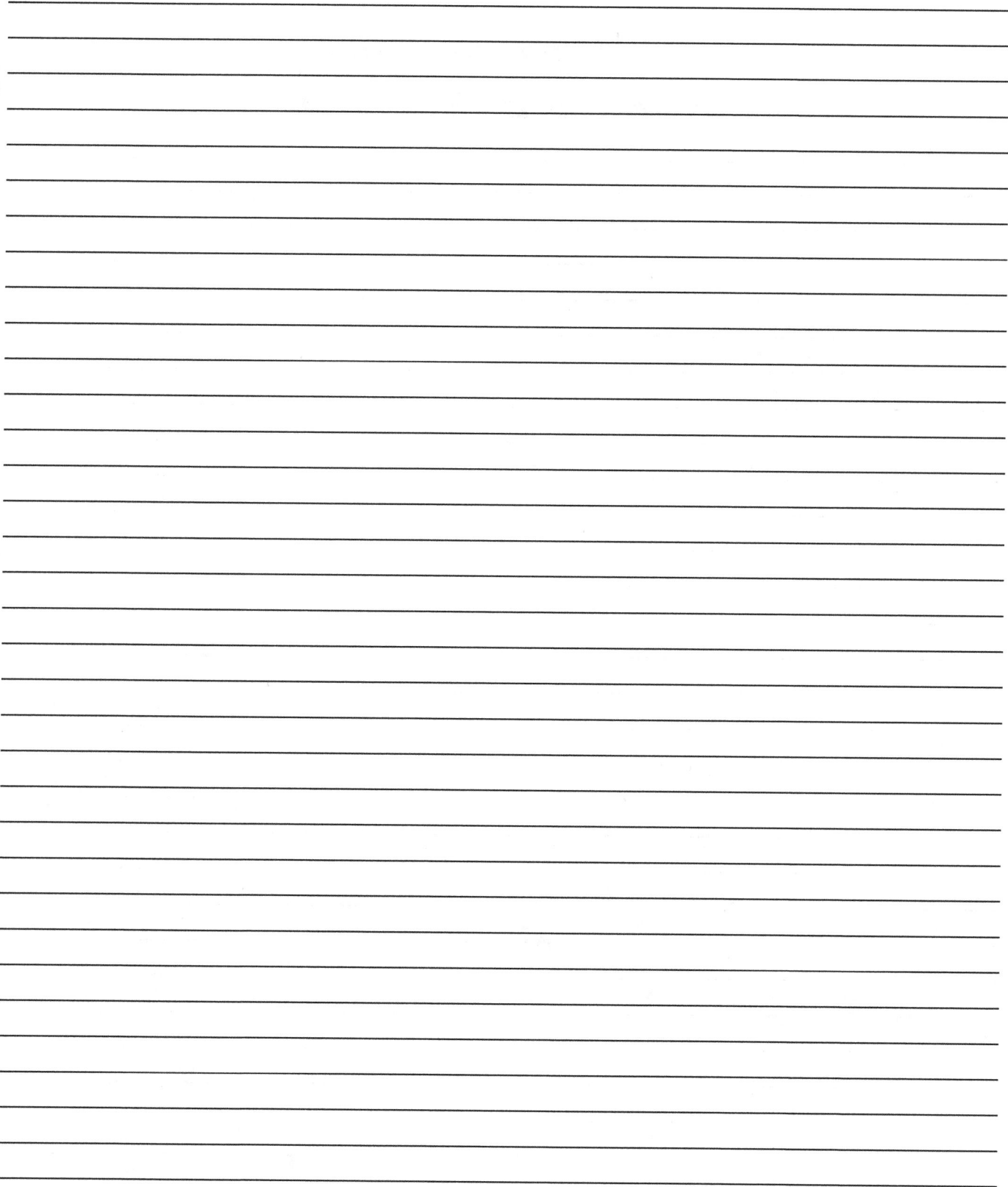

A Prayer of Praise
Going to a New level

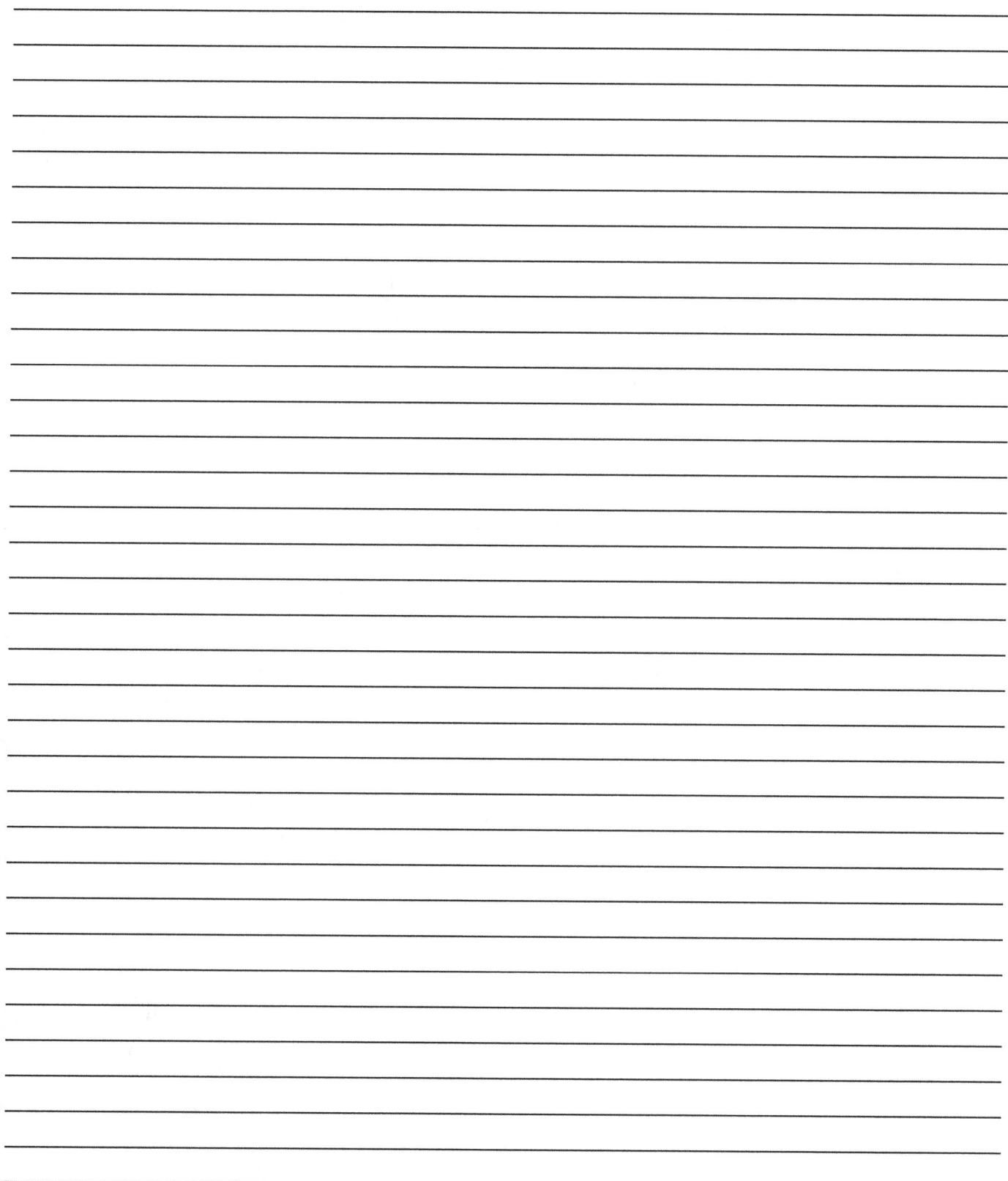

Sing to the Lord a New Song

A Prayer of Agreement

A Prayer of Forgiveness

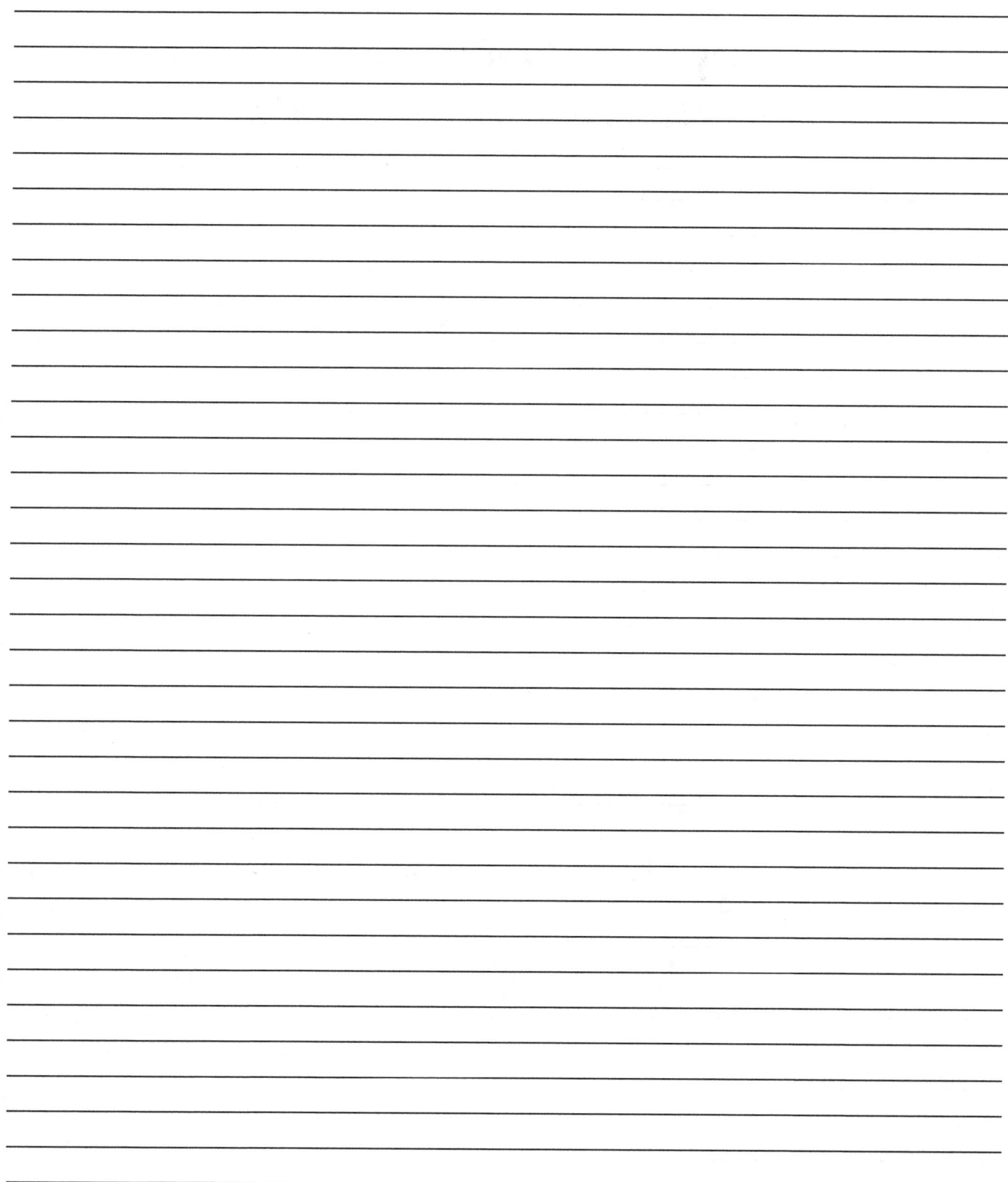

A Prayer of Binding and Loosing
Untie Your Breakthrough

A Prayer Journal

I Am a Women of God
I Am Clothed with Strength and Dignity

I Am a Warrior for God
I Stand with All My Armor On

My Prayers Are Powerful and Are Backed Up by God's Word

The Spirit of Wisdom and Revelation
The Eyes of My Heart Are Being
Enlightened by God's Word

A Prayer Journal
My Love Letter to God

A Prayer Journal
Prayers of Forgiveness

The Eye of the Prophetic
Prophetic Dreams and Insights

Prophetic Dreams God Has Given Me

Date:

_____

_____

_____

_____

_____

_____

_____

_____

_____

_____

_____

_____

_____

_____

_____

_____

_____

_____

_____

_____

_____

_____

_____

_____

_____

_____

_____

_____

_____

_____

_____

_____

Prophetic Visions

Music and the Holy Spirit:
Songs God Has Given Me

Visions

Date:

Time:

What Did They Mean?

Bible Verse:

About the Author

Debby Gautreaux is an intercessor from Baton Rouge, Louisiana. She is a speaker and glory carrier, and God uses her to help other women to have a more effective prayer life through His Word, music, and teachings. She has been married to Russell Gautreaux, PhD for seven years.

Russell Gautreaux teaches seminars on inner and emotional healing, and God has healed many people in their emotions. He has a book called *"The Value of a Broken Vessel."* Between them, they have 5 children and 6 grandchildren. Jeffrey Robillard, Jennifer Forsey, Rachel Byrd, Deborah and Mathew Gautreaux.

You may contact Debby at Belovedroses3@aol.com.